Richard Grant White

Book of the prophet Stephen, son of Douglas

Wherein marvellous things are foretold of the reign of Abraham

Richard Grant White

Book of the prophet Stephen, son of Douglas
Wherein marvellous things are foretold of the reign of Abraham

ISBN/EAN: 9783337102623

Printed in Europe, USA, Canada, Australia, Japan

Cover: Foto ©Lupo / pixelio.de

More available books at **www.hansebooks.com**

BOOK

OF THE

PROPHET STEPHEN,

SON OF DOUGLAS.

WHEREIN MARVELLOUS THINGS ARE FORETOLD OF THE REIGN
OF ABRAHAM.

NEW YORK:

FEEKS & BANCKER,

WHOLESALE NEWSDEALERS AND BOOKSELLERS,

No. 26 ANN STREET.

W. H. TINSON, Stereotyper.   JOHN J. REED, Printer.

PROPHECIES OF STEPHEN,

SON OF DOUGLAS.

——•◦•——

CHAPTER I.

1 *James the Eunich retireth and Abraham the Honest reigneth in his stead.* 3 *King of Woolly-heads, a mighty statesman, splitteth rails and cooketh woodchucks.* 4 *He journeyeth from the Far West.* 6 *He resteth at the City of Gotham; offereth to kiss a fair maiden.* 9 *His deeds of unknown valor.* 10 *He calleth William to be his trumpeter.* 11 *Maketh a fish his "purse bearer," who maketh precious coins out of green paper.* 13 *Simon the Just Minister of Peace.* 13 *A Well he putteth over the sea.* 14 *Father of many children expoundeth the law according to the will of the king.* 19 *A great commotion in the land.* 21 *The inhabitants of Sunland strive for peace but the worshippers of the woolly-headed Dragon refuse.* 24 *A man cometh out of the Tombs and smiteth the altars of the Temple.* 25 *A man getteth drunk and bloweth up the king with a firecracker.* 24 *Abraham coveteth the head of Jeff.* 27 *Sendeth the Pope to slay him with bulls.* 28 *Sends his fiery dragon Burnside.* 29 *Hooker the king's angler goeth forth.* 31 *Orders Park the Post Boy to blow off the heads of* 40,000 *with his horn.* 33 *Abraham is deceived by his cunning counsellors.*

I. It came to pass in the eighty and fourth year of the Republic, that James the Eunich having ruled all the days of his appointed time, retired to the shades of Wheatland, and Abraham, called the Rail-splitter, reigned in his stead.

II. Now Abraham was a child of promise, and a man after the woolly-headed Dragon's own heart; full of exceeding cunning, and beautiful to look upon, as the skin of a sheep drawn over the skeleton of a gorilla.

III. Moreover he was a mighty statesman, having, withal, had much experience in the matter of rail-splitting, flatboating, and cooking woodchucks in the Indian wars.

IV. And behold it came to pass that, on his journey from the Far West to the seat of empire, even to the place that is called the Capitol, he made divers and sundry speeches, of great and marvellous power, insomuch that the hills trembled at the sound of his voice, and vast scores of little pigs, and jackasses, and other beasts of the field, came and gathered about him, and were dumb with amazement at the beauty and majesty of the king.

V. And, lo, when he was come to the place that is called Gotham, that is built upon the water that is over against the land of the Jerseys, he rested for the night. And the people came unto him, and took him up into the temple of the city, and there gathered about him men of high and low degree, who were curious to look upon the king, to see what manner of man he was.

VI. And the great height of Abraham amazed the people, insomuch that a young and daring giant from the Aroostook in the land of Maine, boldly challenged the king to stand up and measure with him. But the king, looking down with pity upon the young man, said, No, I will not measure with thee, but if thou hast a sister, bring her hither, and her I will kiss.

VII. And, lo, the people were dumfounded at the elegance and majesty of the king, and they fell down and worshipped him.

VIII. And Abraham was also a great general, being

a man mighty in battle, and of such exceeding strategy and invisible courage, that he cut his way, by night, through a hundred millions of hostile men in arms, that lay encamped in the region of country that is between the city that is called Harrisburg, and Washington, which is so named from the Father of his Country.

IX. Now, having escaped the bloody legions of his imaginary foes, Abraham ascended the throne on the fourth day of the third month ; and he summoned together the chiefs of his clan, even the mighty men of unknown valor and virtue, who gladly came unto him and threw themselves at his feet.

X. And the king said unto William, whose surname is Seward, come thou and be my chief trumpeter to blow the fame of our kingdom to the four corners of the globe, and to make all other kings and potentates to tremble and flee away before the majesty of our power.

XI. And then he called a fish from the great deep, which is also called *Salmon*, being named Chase among the natives of the wilderness of Ohio, and he said unto him, be thou my purse-bearer ; and as we have neither silver nor gold, get thou engravers and printers, and blue ink, and red ink, and much green paper, and many mighty printing machines withal, and let us print money, to astonish the heathen, who think that nothing but silver and gold are precious metals.

XII. And next the king appointed Simon, who is called *the Just*, to be his minister of peace, and he said unto him, Do thou set up our comely black Idol, and bid all the people to fall down and worship it ; lo, if any refuse, do thou draw forth thy sword, and smite them hip and thigh ; for I say unto you that of

such neither man, woman, nor child shall live in my
kingdom. And Simon bowed down his head, and
kissed the hem of the king's garment, and said, My
lord, I will.

XIII. Then Abraham sent for one Gideon, whose
surname is *Wells*, who is not deep, but is covered
up with much hair, and he said unto him, Do thou be
my ruler over the seas; and get thee speedily a hundred ships, and prepare thyself to lock up three
thousand miles of the coast of the heathen who worship white deities, lest it enter into their heads that
they will not fall down before our comely black Idol.
And Gideon lifted up his beard, and opened his
mouth, and said, O king, thy will shall be done.

XIV. And after this the king sent abroad into the
Far West, and summoned into his presence the father
of many children, who is called Bates, and said unto
him, Come hither, and sit by my side, and be thou
the expounder of my laws, which thou shalt interpret
according to my will, and not after the fashion of the
books and judges which were before in this land.
And the father of many children said, Yea, O king,
thy will is the law.

XV. Now there dwelt in the land the son of Blair,
who was called Montgomery, and the king said unto
his servants, Send hither this man to me, that I may
make him the chief ruler over all my carriers, who
are to do my will in sending forth such papers as are
pleasing unto me, and in putting under their feet
whatever is opposed to the worship of the comely
black Idol. And the father of the Blairs joyfully
sent forth his son, even Montgomery, his youngest
born, to do the bidding of the king.

XVI. And, lo, when all these things were done according to the pleasure of Abraham the king, he

again opened his mouth and said, Now let us have one more man to serve in our name, in the interior of our kingdom; and again he sent forth into the West, and found him a man after his own heart; and when he had appointed him Minister of the Interior he journeyed so far into the interior that his name and his exploits have not been heard of, no, not even to this day.

XVII. And it came to pass in those days that there was a mighty murmuring among the people that dwelt towards the South, and they loudly demanded of the king that he should make known to them, and to all the land, whether they were to be treated as equals in the family of States, or whether the religion of the woolly-headed Dragon and the black Idol were to be the law of the land.

XVIII. Whereupon the king was filled with exceeding dignity, insomuch that he swelled up to four times the size that was convenient to his skin. But he answered not a word, neither would he condescend to have any intercourse with the heathen who worship white deities.

XIX. And when the land was full of trouble, and the hearts of wise men were smitten with dread, the mighty men of the nation came together, from the North and from the South, from the East and from the West, and sat down in council together, as was the custom in those days. But the black fiend had taken possession of the people that dwelt in the Northland, so that they could do nothing to appease the fiery anger of the people that inhabited the region that lies to the south of the city that is called Washington.

XX. Now there were wise and good men in those days, who said, Let us go forth to save our country, that the men of the North and they of the South may still dwell together in unity, for our fathers were brethren.

XXI. And the wise men of the South stood up in the council of the nation, and said, I pray you let us settle this, our trouble, in peace. You men of the North take for yourselves and your black Idol, all the land that lies to the west of the line that is called after the old name of Missouri, that runneth even to the shores of the Pacific Ocean ; and we men of the South will take the little of the public domain that lieth to the south of that line: and we will dwell together as our fathers did, buying and selling and being one people forever and ever.

XXII. These things did John, surnamed Crittenden, a mighty man from the Southland of Kentucky, offer to the inhabitants of the North, in the name of the people of the South.

XXIII. But, lo, the warriors of King Abraham all stood up as one man, and smote their breasts, and tore out their hair, and made such noises as time affordeth not to mention, swearing withall, that they would have peace on no terms that did not ensure the universal worship of the comely black Idol.

XXIV. And in those days came a man out of the *Tombs*, from the South, and smote the altars in the temple of the Nation with his fist, swearing that they of the South and of the North should be two people forever.

XXV. And there followed after him a crazy man, who was called *Wigfall*, because he was often drunken, insomuch that he lost the natural equilibrium of his body, and suffered the artificial covering to his *cranium* to fall prone to the ground. He, too, was full of wrath, and threatened to blow up the king with a fire-cracker.

XXVI. But the greatest of the chiefs of the South was the son of Davis, who was called Jeff, whose *head* the king coveted ; for he showed himself great in skill to govern, and wonderful in the arts of war.

XXVII. Insomuch that when the king sent forth the Pope to devour the hosts of Jeff, and to eat them up alive, according to the bulls he should publish against them, they neither feared, nor did they stand in awe, but came out in great force, and caused the Pope to flee for his life ; and the place was thereafter called Bull Run, by reason of the marvellous flight of the Pope.

XXVIII. And Abraham was discomforted ; but, nothing daunted, he commanded his fiery Dragon, which was called *Burnside*, to go forth and burn up the armies of the heathen, that worship white deities, root and branch. And, behold, when the fiery Dragon, even the all-destroying *Burnside*, was come into their country, they threw great tanks of cold water upon him, insomuch that they utterly quenched him ; so that he came back like a drowned chicken, and roosted in a chamber in the palace of the king.

XXIX. Now the king bethought himself of a terrible and mighty angler among his warriors, which was called *Hooker*, because that he knew how to *hook;* and him he sent forth, saying, Get thee over into the land of the heathen, and put me a hook into the noses of all the rebels, and lead them hither unto me, that I may kill them, every one, and be avenged of the wrongs that they have done unto me.

XXX. And when he had reached the southmost bank of the river that is called Chickahominy, the heathen looked upon him and saw what manner of man he was, and they laughed one to another ; and, in their evil conceits, they sent forth an army of *boots,*

that kicked the hindermost parts of the king's fighting
angler, and drove his rear guard even into the trenches
that lie before the gates of the temple of the Dragon.

XXXI. Now Abraham, the king, was sore oppressed,
because the heathen had kicked the hindermost parts
of his mighty fighting angler; and he smote the earth
until it quaked. And then he called unto him his faithful *Post*-boy, who is called Park, the son of Godwin,
and he said unto him: The heathen have despised the
Pope, and they have quenched my mighty, flaming
Dragon, that is called *Burnside*, and they have kicked
the hindermost parts of *Hooker*, the king's own angler ;
now, therefore, do thou bring forth thine horn, and
point its larger end straight at the heathen, and blow
me a blast that shall blow off the heads of forty thousand.

XXXII. Now, the king's *Post*-boy was mighty of
wind, so that he did even as he was bidden by the
king; and, lo, he blew such a blast on his horn as
astounded the heathen, yea, as blew the seat of his
own nether garment into a thousand pieces, yea, into
a hundred thousand pieces; and the like of it was
never known, no, not since the beginning of the
world.

XXXIII. And, behold, when the king saw that his
mighty, windy *Post*-boy had not blown off the head of
a single rebel, but instead thereof had blown himself
to pieces, he was full of great grief, and of great
wrath, and, lifting up his eyes to the heavens, he exclaimed: Art thou, then, in the name of a thousand
devils, on the side of the heathen ? and is it thus that
thou fightest for the comely black Idol, even for thine
own church of the woolly-headed Dragon ?

XXXIV. And Abraham was smitten with amazement because his warriors had told him that speedily,

yea, in ninety days, the hosts of the heathen should be blown away, as chaff before a mighty North wind; and, behold, nothing had come to pass according to the promise of his cunning counsellors and many mighty warriors. So Abraham hid his face in his mantle and was ashamed.

———•••———

CHAPTER II.

2 *Stephen the Prophet standeth up in the temple, and denounceth the worshippers of the woolly-headed Dragon—he showeth that they want war.* 3 *The worshippers of the Dragon gnash their teeth at the Prophet.* 5 *The warriors of the king shed the blood of millions in their speeches.* 6 *They fain would destroy the Prophet by the blowing of rams' horns.* 7 *The Prophet showeth them that war is disunion.* 8 *He chargeth them with a design to destroy their country.* 9 *He proveth that all tyrants set up their claim to prove that they* have a government. 10 *The Prophet showeth that a wise nation goeth not to war with its own people.* 11 *He showeth that the chief government hath no right to use the army, except according to law, to aid the civil power.* 12 *He telleth the truth concerning Fort Sumter.* 13 *He proveth that Peace is the only policy that can save the country.*

I. Now just before those days appeared Stephen the Prophet, who was also called Douglas, a mighty man in the councils of the nation, and beloved of the people; but hated by the king, because he had met him in the Westland, where the Prophet had proclaimed aloud the abominations of the woolly-headed Dragon, named by King Abraham—*the comely black Idol.*

II. And Stephen the Prophet stood up in the council of the nation, even in the Senate chamber, and, pointing his finger at the partisans of the king, cried out with a loud voice, saying: *You want war, because you*

*think that war will drive off the South and leave every-
thing here to the mercy of your hands.*

III. And the partisans of the king, even Sumner, the pupil of Demosthenes, who stealeth the orations of his master, and Wade, called by Vallandigham *the coward* who *wadeth* up to his loins in the blood he hath not the pluck to shed himself, and all the hosts of the king, gnashed their teeth at the Prophet, and fain would have stoned him, but that they knew that the people loved him.

IV. And the king was exceeding wroth, and sent for his chief warriors, even for William Pitt, who was called Fessenden, from the land of Maine, and said unto him, This seditious Stephen the Prophet is an offence unto me. He has been my evil genius even in the land of Illinois, where he proclaimed these infamous words in my own ears: "*I hold that this Government was made on the* WHITE BASIS, *by* WHITE MEN, *for the benefit of* WHITE MEN, *and their* POSTERITY, *forever.*" Therefore, O ye warriors of mine, be sure that some-how you bring to naught this stiff-necked prophet, him and his doctrines.

V. Then all the fuglemen of the king, even the val-liant warriors who shed the blood of millions of men in their speeches in the temple, put their heads together to see how they should confound Stephen the Prophet.

VI. And, lo, they agreed that they would bring him down, as the walls of Jericho were brought down, by the blowing of rams' horns; and straightway they all began to blow at Stephen, until a mighty roaring wind shook the windows of the temple, and filled the spec-tators with fear, insomuch that fair women left the galleries in much trembling, and the old men said that such things had not been seen, no, not since the begin-ning of the Republic.

VII. Now, after all these things, Stephen came forth and opened his mouth and said unto them, Do you think to confound the people with noise? Do you hope to save the Union by war? Verily, I say unto you that

"*War is disunion. War is final, eternal separation. Hence, disguise it as you may, every Union man in America must advocate such amendments to the Constitution as will preserve peace and restore the Union; while every disunionist, whether openly or secretly plotting its destruction, is the advocate of peaceful secession, or of war, as the surest means of rendering reunion and reconstruction impossible. I have too much respect for any man that has standing enough to be elected a Senator, to believe that he is for war, as a means for preserving the Union, I have too much respect for his intellect to believe, for one moment, that there is a man for war who is not a disunionist per se. Hence I do not mean, if I can prevent it, that the enemies of the Union—men plotting to destroy it— shall drag this country into war under the pretext of protecting the public property, and enforcing the laws, and collecting revenue, when their object is disunion, and war the means of accomplishing a cherished purpose.*"

VIII. And while Stephen thus spake, the followers of the woolly-headed Dragon, even the warriors of the king, were filled full of anger as a coal, yea, as a-live coal is of fire, and they raved at him; but Stephen heeded not their anger, neither did he fear them, but continued saying unto them:

"*The disunionists, therefore, are divided into two classes; the one open, the other secret disunionists. The one in favor of peaceful secession and a recognition of independence; the other is in favor of war, as the surest means of accomplishing the object, and of making the separation final, eternal.   I am a Union man, and hence against war.*"

IX. Behold, when the Prophet had uttered these words, the Pitt of the Senate chamber was stirred up with exceeding wrath, and demanded to know if the king should not stretch forth his hand, even the hand of his power, to show that there is a government in this land?   And the Prophet answered the clamors of the Pitt, saying :

"*But we are told, and we hear it repeated everywhere, that we must find out if we have got a government. 'Have we a government?' is the question; and we are told we must test that question by using the military power to put down all discontented spirits. Sir, this question, 'have we a government?' has been pronounced by every tyrant who has tried to keep his feet on the necks of the people since the world began. When the barons demanded Magna Charta from King John, at Runnymede, he exclaimed, 'have we a government?' and called for his army to put down the discontented barons. When Charles I. attempted to collect the ship money in violation of the constitution of England, and in disregard of the rights of the people, and was resisted by them, he exclaimed, 'have we a government?   We cannot treat with rebels; put down the traitors; we must show that we have a government.' When James II. was driven from the throne of England for trampling on the liberties of the people, he called for his army, and exclaimed, 'let us show that we have a government!' When George III. called upon his army to put down the rebellion in America, Lord North cried lustily, 'no compromise with traitors; let us demonstrate that we have a government.' When, in 1848, the people rose upon their tyrants all over Europe, and demanded guarantees for their rights, every crowned head exclaimed, 'have we a government?' and appealed to the army to vindicate their authority and to enforce the law.*[1]

X. Now these words of the Prophet Stephen only the more stirred up the worshippers of the black Idol to an evil and revengeful spirit, but he continued to rebuke them, saying :

" *Sir, the history of the world does not fail to condemn the folly, weakness, and wickedness of that government which drew its sword upon its own people when they demanded guarantees for their rights. This cry, that we must have a government, is merely following the example of the besotted Bourbon, who never learned anything by misfortune, never forgave an injury, never forgot an affront. Must we demonstrate that we have got a government, and coerce obedience without reference to the justice or injustice of the complaints? Sir, whenever ten million people proclaim to you, with one unanimous voice, that they apprehend their rights, their firesides, and their family altars are in danger, it becomes a wise government to listen to the appeal, and to remove the apprehension. History does not record an example where any human government has been strong enough to crush ten million people into subjection when they believe their rights and liberties were imperiled, without first converting the government itself into a despotism, and destroying the last vestige of freedom.*

· " *Let us take warning from the examples of the past. Wherever a government has refused to listen to the complaints of the people, and attempted to put down their murmurs by the bayonet, they have paid the penalty.*"

XI. Moreover, said the Prophet, continuing to ex-

pose the wickedness or foolishness of the unlawful
plans of the king and his warriors:

*"But we are told that the President is going to
enforce the laws in the seceded States. How? By
calling out the militia and using the army and navy!
These terms are used as freely and as flippantly as if·
we were a military government where martial law was
the only rule of action, and the will of the monarch
was the only law on the subject. Sir, the President
cannot use the army, or the navy, or the militia, for
any purpose not authorized by law. What is that? If
there be an insurrection in any State against laws and
authorities thereof, the President can use the military
to put it down only when called upon by the State
Legislature, if it be in session, or, if it cannot be con-
vened, by the Governor. He cannot interfere except
when requested. If, on the contrary, the insurrection
be against the laws of the United States instead of a
State, then the President can use the military only as
a posse comitatus in aid of the marshal in such cases
as are so extreme that judicial authority and the powers
of the marshal cannot put down the obstruction. The
military cannot be used in any case whatever except in
the aid of civil process to assist the marshal to execute
a writ."*

XII. And when Stephen had finished these words,
he opened his mouth again to persuade the worship-
ers of the woolly-headed Dragon, that they should
make satisfaction to the men that dwell in Sunland,
saying:

*"If we consider this question calmly, and make such
amendments as will convince the people of the Southern
States that they are safe and secure in their person, in
their property, and in their family relations, within
the Union, we can restore and preserve it. If we can-*

*not satisfy the people of the border States that they may
remain in the Union with safety, dissolution is inevi-
table. Then the simple question comes back, what shall
be the policy of the Union men of this country? Shall
it be peace, or shall it be war? What man in all
America, with a heart in his bosom, who knows the
facts connected with Fort Sumter, can hesitate in saying that duty, honor, patriotism, humanity, require
that Anderson and his gallant band should be instantly
withdrawn? Sir, I am not afraid to say so. I would
scorn to take a party advantage or manufacture parti-
san capital out of an act of patriotism."*

XIII. And thus the Prophet pleaded that they
should be at peace with their brethren in Sunland :

*" Peace is the only policy that can save the country.
Let peace be proclaimed as the policy, and you will
find that a thrill of joy will animate the heart of every
patriot in the land ; confidence will be restored ; busi-
ness will be revived ; joy will gladden every heart ;
bonfires will blaze upon the hill-tops and in the valleys,
and the church bells will proclaim the glad tidings in
every city, town and village in America, and the
applause of a grateful people will greet you everywhere.
Proclaim the policy of war, and there will be gloom
and sadness and despair pictured upon the face of every
patriot in the land. A war of kindred, family and
friends ; father against son, mother against daughter,
brother against brother, to subjugate one-half of this
country into obedience to the other half ; if you do not
mean this, if you mean peace, let this be adopted, and
give the President the opportunity, through the Secre-
tary of War, to speak the word ' peace ;' and thirty
million people will bless him with their prayers, and
honor him with their shouts of joy."*

XIV. And these were the last words spoken by the

Prophet in the council of the nation; for he never returned more to behold the abomination of desolation which should fall upon its altars, by reason of the treason and brutishness of the worshippers of the Dragon.

———•••——— .

CHAPTER III.

1 The Prophet retireth to his own hired house and teacheth the people that come unto him. 2 The Angel of Peace appeareth unto him and showeth the abominations of the woolly-headed Dragon. 4 He prophesieth of the desolation of the land. 7 The Angel of Peace showeth him out of the Prophet Jeremiah that an evil shall spring out of the North that shall spoil the whole land. 10 He showeth from Jeremiah that the pastors of the churches shall become brutish, and be destroyed. 11 He showeth that the people shall take vengeance of the false judges. 12 He showeth out of Jeremiah that the judges shall become false and judge not according to the law, but according to the will of the king. 14 He prophesieth that the abomination of desolation shall last as long as Abraham ruleth.

I. AND, behold, when Stephen had denounced the strong men, and all the warriors of the woolly-headed Dragon in the temple, he went apart by himself into a secret place, even into his own hired house. And there came much people unto him, such as were of pure heart and loved the land of their fathers, and he opened his mouth and taught them, saying:

II. Harken unto me, O ye people; for at mid-day the Angel of Peace came down with a great light out of the heavens, and said unto me: Stephen, the son of Douglas, what seest thou? And I said, I see a woolly-headed Dragon, whose tail and hindermost parts are in the North, but from his mouth goeth out forked lightnings and hot flame, that rageth even towards the South.

III. Again a great rushing light came before my eyes, and the Angel of Peace said, What seest thou? And I said: I see a *seething-pot*, and around about it standing the giants of Abraham, the mighty king of the Woolly-heads.

IV. Then the Angel smote the cloud of smoke with his rod, and said: Behold, O Stephen, the seething-pot is thy country, and the giants round about, even the warriors of the woolly-headed Dragon, shall ravage thy fields and bring desolation and famine upon all the land. There shall not be one stone in the foundations of the Temple of Liberty that shall not be thrown down. Neither *habeas corpus*, nor trial by jury, nor any other thing that thy fathers gave thee shall be left for thee and for thy children, so long as Abraham, the king of the Woolly-heads, reigneth.

V. And thy sons shall be slain in battle, their children shall cry for bread, and the mourners shall go about the streets, when there shall be none to pity them; for the woolly-headed Dragon shall harden the hearts of his people, that they shall not hear the cries of the widows and the orphans that they have made.

VI. And in those days beggars, and such as are called thieves, shall become rich men. They shall wax fat, and kick at whomsoever will not fall down and worship the black Idol. So they that were beggars and serving men shall dwell in palaces, and shall fill their bellies with strong drinks and hot meats, and swell up with great pride and much wind, until they shall be known in the whole region round about for their insolence and much stinking.

VII. Then about the second hour of the third watch of the night the Angel of Peace came unto me the

second time, holding a Bible in his hand, and he
opened to the book of the Prophet Jeremiah, and said
unto me, Read; and I opened my eyes and read these
words: "Then said the Lord unto me, out of the North
an evil shall break forth upon all the inhabitants of
the land."

VIII. And the Angel turned over a leaf in the book
of the Prophecy of Jeremiah, and said unto me, Now
open thine eyes and read what thou seest; and I be-
held these words: "My bowels, my bowels! I am
pained at my very heart; my heart maketh a noise in
me; I cannot hold my peace, because thou hast heard,
O my soul, the sound of the trumpet, the alarm of
war. Destruction upon destruction is cried, for the
whole land is spoiled; suddenly are my tents spoiled,
and my curtains in a moment. For my people is foolish, they have not known me; they are sottish children, and they have none understanding; they are wise
to do evil, but to do good they have no knowledge.
And when thou art spoiled, what wilt thou do? Though
thou clothest thyself with crimson, though thou deck-
est thee with ornaments of gold—thy lovers will despise thee, they will seek thy life."

IX. And then I said in my heart, Behold, O my
people, in these words of the Prophet Jeremiah, what
woe shall be visited upon this our land, because of the
rule of Abraham and the giants of the woolly-headed
Dragon.

X. Again the Angel of Peace turned over a leaf in
the book of the Prophet Jeremiah, and said unto me,
Open thine eyes and read, and I read: "The priests
said not, where is the Lord? the pastors transgressed
against me, and the prophets prophesied by Baal, and
walked after things that do not profit. For the pastors are become brutish, and have not sought the Lord ;

therefore they shall not prosper, and their flocks shall be scattered."

XI. And, lo, when I read these things out of the Prophet Jeremiah, my heart was sore within me, and mine eyes were full of tears, for I knew that the priests of this land should become brutish, that the blessed altars of peace should be changed into butcher's shambles, and war, revenge and blood should stream forth from the desecrated places of religion. By reason of these things I saw that the churches should be broken up, and that the sons of Anack and Belial, who are also called after the names of Beecher, Cheever and Tyng, should corrupt the hearts of the pastors, until they all become *brutish* together, and walk in the fiery paths with the children of perdition. Verily I say unto you, the end of these wolves in sheep's clothing shall be that of the ungodly, and their names shall be stricken out of the Book of Life. Their carcasses shall be devoured by the eagles, and the young eagles shall pick out their eyes; the bittern shall eat the flesh of their bones, and the lizzard shall hatch its young in the hollow of their skulls. For they have not harkened to the voice of peace, neither would they heed the commandments of the Prince of Peace.

XII. And I lifted up my eyes, and behold, the Angel of Peace was still standing before me, with the first finger of his right hand pointing to another passage in the book of the Prophecy of Jeremiah, and he commanded me to read, and I read these words: "And they that handle the law know me not." And the Angel dropt his head upon his breast and wept.

XIII. Then, ah woe is me, I knew that the judges of this land would also be led astray by the *green charms* of the woolly-headed Dragon, and that they would no longer judge according to the law and the

testimony, as was the custom of our fathers, but according to the will of the king.

XIV. And when I lifted up my eyes, behold the
Angel still was weeping, and his face was bowed even
to the ground; which showed unto me that this the
corruption of the judges of the land was the sorest
calamity that could overtake a free people. Then I
cried aloud in my despair. I said : O Lord, is this
people lost? How long shall the perjured judges escape the vengeance of the people? How long are
these days of our humiliation and shame? And suddenly there appeared a black cloud before my eyes,
in the midst of which these words were written in let-
ters as red as flame: *"Behold, as long as Abraham
and the woolly-headed Dragon bear rule."*

XV. And I said, How long, O Angel of Peace, shall
it be to the end of these days of our abomination, even
to the end of the rule of Abraham and the worshippers of the black Idol? Then the Angel lifted up his
head, and I saw that his eyes were sad, and sorrow
covered his face as a garment, but he answered not a
word; and, behold, in the midst of a great and shining
light he ascended up into the heavens, and I covered
my face with my mantle, for I was sore with grief and
stricken in heart with much grief.

CHAPTER IV.

2 *The Prophet showeth out of the Book of Jeremiah that the woolly-headed Dragon shall put a lying spirit into the minds of the people. 4 The worshippers of the black Idol shall persecute and imprison the worshippers of the white deities. 5 The hypocrites shall leave the temple of the white deities, and go out into the temple of the black Idol, and come back loaded with the green jewels of the Dragon. 6 Daniel, the son of Dick, shall get into a den of thieves. 8 The building of the new Temple of Janus half way between the temple of the white deities and that of the black Idol—Peter, the son of Cagger, and the Dean of Richmond. 9 Elijah, the War Horse turned into a donkey in the dirt-carts of the King. 11 The ruler of the Knickerbockers ascendeth like an eagle and lighteth like a dove—The Dean of Richmond buildeth him a chicken-coop behind the Temple of Janus. 12. The people shall plot to destroy the Temple of Janus.*

I. Now it came to pass on the third day of the sixth month, at about the middle of the first watch of the night, that the Angel of Peace came unto me the third time, bearing in his hand the book of the Prophet Jeremiah, which was open at the seventh chapter, and he said unto me, Arise, O Stephen, the son of Douglas, for I have that for thee to read that shall tell thee what is to befall thy land before the end of the reign of Abraham the king of the Woolly-heads.

II. Then I arose, and looked into the book of the prophet that was in the hand of the Angel, and read these words: " But thou shalt say unto them that this is a nation that obeyeth not the voice of the Lord their God, nor receiveth correction: truth is perished, and is cut off from their mouth. And they bend their tongues like their bows for lies."

III. And then I knew, O my people, that the fol

lowers of the woolly-headed Dragon should destroy
and utterly spoil this land with their lying tongues,
which should breed evil surmisings, and discontent,
and slanderous reports, and all manner of lying
abominations, until there should be no soundness, no,
nor any truth left among the people.

IV. Moreover, it appeared unto my vision, that
the worshippers of the black Idol shall persecute
and say all manner of things falsely against the worshippers of the white deities; insomuch that they shall
be stoned in the streets, and be led to prison to be
devoured of the vermin of the woolly-headed Dragon,
and suffer violence at the hands of the Woolly-heads,
because they will not fall down to worship the black
Idol of the king.

V. And in those days fearfulness shall seize upon
all the hypocrites that have crept for a cover into the
temple of the white deities, and they shall run out in
the train of the woolly-headed Dragon, and shall prostrate themselves before the black Idol, and swear like
that Judas whose bowels gushed out, that they never
knew the white deities. And these shall come back
loaded with the *green charms* of the woolly-headed
Dragon.

VI. And the greatest of the apostates from the
temple of the white deities shall be Daniel, the son
of Dick; not that Daniel that was in the lion's den,
but that other Daniel, that got himself into a den of
thieves, and took the Scriptures down with him, and
quoted them, to the great delight of the harlequins
that dance before the black Idol in the temple of the
Dragon.

VII. Now in those days many shall fall away from
the truth by reason of fear, who shall not go over to
the temple of the woolly-headed Dragon, nor will
they dare to remain wholly in the temple of the white

deities, but shall go out midway between the two, and shall make their benedictions first to the one and then to the other, looking two ways at the same time, like the heathen gods in the temple of Janus.

VIII. Among such as these shall be Peter, not that Peter who denied his master once in Judea, but Peter, the son of Cagger, who denied his principles a thousand times in the land of the Knickerbockers; and with him also the great Dean of Richmond, called the Profane, of whose riches and cunning manœuvering there is no end; and these shall build a new temple of Janus, and many are they that shall come therein to worship.

IX. And these shall take Elijah, called the *War Horse*, and they shall turn him into a *donkey*, and shall make him to draw dirt in the dirt-carts of Abraham the king of the Woolly-heads, whereby they shall get great gain to themselves, and shall enrich themselves, even with the *green charms* of the Dragon.

X. Now a great ruler shall arise in those days, to whom the people shall look for deliverance from the power of the Dragon, and to him shall be given the name of *See More*, because it shall be believed that he hath the gift of seeing further than other men, even than the cunning king Abraham, of whose wisdom no man shall know, no, not to the end of time.

XI. And this great ruler shall rise before the people like a mighty eagle, and he shall soar proudly up, and fly very high, and spread his broad wings over the whole continent, insomuch that there shall be a great fluttering among the chickens of the Dragon; but when the king of the Woolly-heads, who is a cunning archer, shall come forth with his bow and arrow, this proud eagle shall subside as gently as a cooing dove, and gracefully light in a chicken-coop, which the great Dean of Richmond shall cause to be built a hundred and twenty cubits back of the new temple of Janus.

XII. Lo, there shall be great murmuring and much indignation among the people, and they shall smite their breasts and demand, Who shall deliver us from the power of the Dragon, and from the tyranny of Abraham the king of the Woolly-heads? And they shall plan among themselves how they shall destroy the new temple of Janus, by means of which so many worshippers are drawn away from the temple of the white deities, and carried off half-way over to the temple of the black Idol.

———•••———

CHAPTER V.

1 *The Gothamites shall murmur against their Watchmen because they take bribes from the King of the Woolly-heads.* 2 *They send for See More to come over and help them.* 3 *He sendeth his man Friday,* Waterberry *the Valiant.* 5 *The man Friday gathereth three ship loads of proof against the Watchmen, and See More sweareth that the Watchmen shall die.* 6 *Great joy among the Gothamites—every man kisseth his neighbor's wife for joy.* 7 *The Watchmen escape the vengeance of the Ruler of the Knickerbockers.* 9 *The People murmur and smite the Ruler of the Knickerbockers, because he deceived them.* 10 *The Prophet foretells the death of all the worshippers in the Temple of Janus.* 12 *He warns the people to beware of* The World *which guideth the people into the Temple of Janus, and showeth that its heart is like* Marble, *and its blood like that of a* Halibut. 13 *He warneth against false Judges, such as* Daly *defile the Temple of Justice.* 14 *He warneth against Lawyers who plead for the black Idol for hire.*

I. And in those days shall be great murmuring among the people of Gotham, a city that is builded by the waters over against the land of the Jerseys, because of the impurity and wickedness of their watchmen, who shall rebel against the people their masters, and shall take bribes from the king of the Woolly-heads, by means of which great and scandalous wrongs shall be committed against the liberty and peace of the Gotham-ites.

II. And they shall say to the mighty ruler of the Knickerbockers, who is also called See More, We pray thee to come over and help us, and to defend us and our children from the machinations of the evil dis-posed watchmen, who have sold themselves to the worshipper of the woolly-headed Dragon.

III. And he shall send his man Friday, who is called Waterberry, by reason of his head looking like a small berry growing at the top of a tall water-weed, a man valiant in his own conceit, who shall never be known to covet anything that belongeth not to another, nor to take anything that lieth beyond the reach of his hand, whose honesty no man shall see, nor shall any man comprehend it to the end of time.

IV. Behold, the mighty ruler of the Knickerbockers shall say to this man, Get thee down to the Gotham-ites, and bring me back a faithful record of the abomi-nations of the watchmen, that I may revenge the people of the wrongs that they have suffered at their hands.

V. And, lo, the man Friday, even he that is called Waterberry, shall go down to the city of Gotham, and shall gather up testimony against the faithless watch-men, that shall fill a hundred thousand volumes, and shall take them back in three ships to the ruler of the Knickerbockers, who shall swear in his wrath that the watchmen shall die.

VI. And he shall smite the mountains and they shall tremble at his nod, and the sea shall roar, and the birds of the air shall fall dead with fright; and the people of Gotham shall rejoice with exceeding joy, insomuch that every man shall kiss his neighbor's wife, because they shall be delivered from the hands of the faithless watchmen.

VII. But I say unto you, that the mountains shall tremble, and the sea roar, and the birds die, and the other men's wives shall be kissed in vain, for the watchmen shall not die, neither shall they be driven out by the mighty ruler of the Knickerbockers; for behold, he barketh like a dog, but runneth like a hare.

VIII. And the people shall become sick at heart, for they shall see their hopes perish, and shall find none to deliver them from the hands of Abraham the king, nor from the malice of the worshippers of the woolly-headed Dragon.

IX. And they shall smite the ruler of the Knickerbockers until he die, so that he shall not be king, according to the promise of the worshippers in the temple of Janus.

X. Moreover, I say unto you, that all who follow the hypocrites into the temple of Janus shall die; for they have forsaken the temple of the white deities, and turned their faces away from the altars that were builded by their fathers.

XI. And all the men of this world shall die, because *The World* shall deceive them and lead them astray from the paths of truth, unto the temple of the heathen, even the new temple of Janus.

XII. Give ear and hearken unto me, O ye worshippers of the white deities, be ye not mixed up with the followers of *The World*, for it is a wolf in sheep's clothing; it hath been the herald of the king of the Woolly-heads, and was taken by the Bohemians, for hire, over into the temple of Janus, where it boweth from afar to the white deities, while its heart is far from it. It knoweth not Democracy, neither understandeth it the worship of the white deities, for it hath a heart like *Marble*, and its blood is like that of a *Halibut*.

XIII. Beware, also, of false judges, and such as *Daly* defile the altars of justice with sacrifices to the black Idol by reason of the green charms of the woolly-headed Dragon.

XIV. Moreover, I say unto you, shun the council of lawyers, who sell their country to the black Idol for the green charms of the Dragon. *Brade-he* never so fair a web of cunningly devised falsehoods to hide his treachery to the white deities, believe him not; neither suffer thyself to be drawn into the ways of his footsteps; for his paths are filthy with lucre, and he getteth fat with the fees of sin. From such turn away.

———•◦•———

CHAPTER VI.

1 *The Prophet showeth out of Jeremiah that Benjamin, the king's Butler, shall plunder the City of Orleans. 3 He shall be called the Bruit, and shall treat the mothers of children like harlots. 4 His officers shall take concubines of the Ethiopians, and dwell in the mansions of the rich. 5 The Post-boy of Gotham shall trumpet the praise of Benjamin the Bruit. 6 The King is offended at his Butler because he hordeth the gold which he stealeth—he putteth Nathaniel the dancing-master in his place. 7 The Angel of Peace showeth out of Jeremiah that those who have called green paper money shall die as the fool. 11 He showeth that those who think they have money as a dog hath fleas are without riches. 12 He showeth the people the mountain of debt which the king's purse-bearer shall build. 14 He showeth that the people shall scatter the riches which the worshippers of the Dragon made out of green paper, so that their children shall beg bread in the streets.*

I. Now it came to pass on the seventh day of the eighth month, the same being the fifth month of the reign of Abraham, the son of Inlow, whose mother was of the Ethiopian tribe of Hanks, that the Angel of Peace appeared unto me the fourth time, holding in his left hand the book of the Prophet Jeremiah; and he said unto me, Arise, O Stephen, and make thine eyes familiar with these words of the twentieth chapter and twenty-second verse of the Prophet; and I read after this manner: " Behold, the noise of the *bruit* is come, and a great commotion out of the North country, to make the cities desolate, and a den of dragons. . . When I had fed them to the full, they then committed adultery, and assembled themselves by troops in the harlots' houses. They were as fed horses in the morning; every one neighed after his neighbor's wife. Shall I not visit them for these things? saith the Lord, and shall not my soul be avenged on such a nation as this?"

II. And as I read these words out of the book of the Prophet, lo, the Angel of Peace was sore oppressed, insomuch that his whole frame shook with horror: and then I saw what must befall the city that is called New, and that beareth also the name of Orleans, that is built by the shore of the father of waters, afar off, in the land that lieth to the south of the habitation of the woolly-headed Dragon.

III. And I said, This is a doomed city; for the king of the Woolly-heads, even Abraham, the son of Inlow, shall send Benjamin, his Butler, who shall also be called " the Bruit," as is given in the Prophet Jeremiah; and he shall enter in and dwell there, and the inhabitants thereof shall flee before his hand as from a pestilence; for he shall order his soldiers to go out, every one of them, to plunder the people, and to treat all the fair women, even such as are the mothers of children, as harlots.

IV. Now the officers and soldiers of Benjamin, w is called the Bruit, shall do even as they are b

and they shall drive out the inhabitants from their
own dwellings, and take to themselves comely black
concubines of the Ethiopian tribes that abound in those
regions; and they shall enter into the mansions of the
rich and dwell there, eating and drinking and making
merry in their hearts.

V. And the king's Butler, even Benjamin the Bruit,
shall flourish like a green bay tree, and shall become
rich beyond other men by reason of plundering the
people of the city; and his fame shall spread abroad
throughout the land, even unto Gotham, where a
Post-boy shall trumpet his praise afar to all such as
love much stealing, and to every one that hath a
lickerish tooth towards the fair and fragrant daughters
of Ethiopia.

VI. But it shall come to pass that the king shall
become wroth with Benjamin, his Butler, because,
while he stealeth many hundred pounds of gold, he
cunningly hideth it in his own house, and never bring-
eth, not so much as even one ounce, into the temple
of the woolly-headed Dragon; therefore the king shall
say unto his Butler, Now, get thee out of this city, for
I will no more of thee; and I will put my faithful
servant Nathaniel, the dancing-master, who is the son
of Banks, into thy place, and he shall steal *honestly*,
and shall bring the full half of all the plunder into the
temple of the Dragon.

VII. Now while all these things passed before my
vision a great and sudden trembling seized my whole
frame, and I was stricken with much sorrow; for I saw
that, according to the Prophet Jeremiah, God will one
day " be avenged on such a nation as this," and that
the whole people will be made to suffer for the abominations of Abraham the king and all the besotted wor
shippers in the temple of the Dragon.

VIII. And in the midst of this affliction, even the sorrow that straineth the reins, and maketh the head like waters, the Angel of Peace opened the book of the Prophet Jeremiah, at the eleventh verse of the seventeenth chapter, and commanded me to read.

IX. Behold the words of the Prophet: " As a partridge sitteth on eggs and hatcheth them not, so he that getteth riches, and not by right, shall leave them in the midst of his days, and at his end shall be a fool."

X. And I was sore afraid, for I knew not the meaning of these words, neither could I understand them ; and I spake unto the Angel of Peace, and said: I pray thee to open mine eyes that I may know and understand the words of the Prophet.

XI. Then the Angel opened his mouth and taught me, saying : The days shall come when the land shall be full of green paper, and it shall be called money by the worshippers of the black Idol. And every man shall have a bag full of such as is called money ; yea, the woolly-headed Dragon shall measure out his money to the followers of the king by the hundred yards at a measure ; and they that are drunken and such as spend their days with lewd women, and such as know not how to read, neither can they write, by reason of their great ignorance, shall abound with money as a dog with fleas, yea, as a little dog with many fleas.

XII. And verily I say unto you that the people, whose eyes shall be charmed so that they shall think the green paper to be money, shall allow the king's purse-bearer, even he that shall be called Chase, because the imaginations of his heart shall be *chased* day and night by visions of the fair daughters of Ethiopia, to heap up a great mountain of debt, so that the people can never climb to the top thereof, neither can they dig under it, nor go round it, but it shall be there to devour the substance of them and their children forever and ever.

XIII. Behold, he that thinketh himself rich, by reason of so much green paper, shall be poor, for the day cometh that it shall be naught, and, as saith the Prophet Jeremiah, "at his end he shall be a fool."

XIV. Then harken unto me, O ye fools! for the day cometh that shall burn as an oven, and all ye that have made gain by shoddy, and enriched yourselves by the robbing of the people, shall be burned up by the fierce anger of the people; for I say unto you that hunger breaketh through a stone wall, and that the wealth which you shall steal away from the people, as the unlawful spoils of war, shall be scattered by the hand of the people, to them and to their children, and your own offspring shall beg bread in the street.

——•••——

CHAPTER VII.

1 *The Angel of Peace pronounceth the doom of the worshippers of the black Idol.* 2 *Their sons shall be sent forth to battle and die.* 3 *The warriors of Sunland shall kill them man for man.* 4 *The Angel of Peace showeth that the woolly-headed Dragon had made his worshippers like swine, and not like men.* 5 *Their names shall stink in the nostrils of the nations.* 6 *He foretelleth the doom of the Loyal Leaguers.*

I. Thus saith the Angel of Peace: O ye followers of the woolly-headed Dragon, who hath hardened your hearts that ye cannot feel, who hath blinded your eyes that ye cannot see! For have you not said one to another: Let us gather together our sons, even under

2*

the banners of our fighting men, and send them down
to the dwellers in Sunland, to slay all that will not
bow the knee to the comely black Idol in the temple
of the Dragon!

II. And behold your sons shall go forth and they
shall not return. They shall take the sword and they
shall perish by the sword. The mothers of the land
shall weep for the slain of their offspring; your old
men shall die, waiting for the return of their youngest
born, and there shall be no eye that shall not weep,
no, not from one end of the land to the other.

III. Now, therefore, harken unto me, and give ear
to the words of my saying! To what end do you send
forth your sons to kill the dwellers in Sunland! For
do they not slay your sons, man for man? To what
end do you burn their wheat-fields? To what end do
you steal their cunningly-wrought silver spoons? To
what end do you lie down in the tall grass by the side
of their black wenches? For is it thus that you would
bring them back to sit with us in love as did their
fathers? ·

IV. O ye blind of heart and void of understanding,
who hath delivered you over into this slough of fool- .
ishness? Who hath made you like swine, and not
men? Who hath taught you to forget that you are
white men, and not negroes? Verily I say unto you
that you have debased yourselves, and gone after other
gods, wallowing about in blood and uncleanness.

V. Therefore, saith the Angel of Peace, ye shall
perish in your naughtiness. Ye shall be a by-word
among the nations; yea, and your names shall stink
in the nostrils of the nations; so that there shall be
none that do not abhor you. They shall point at you
in the streets, and shall say: There goeth a fool; yea,
a very fool, and the father of fools!

VI. And ye of the "Loyal Leagues" shall be inflated with ignorance and pride, and shall swell up until ye crack with insolence and much stuffing, so that they of clean lives shall run from you, and hold their noses at your passing. Verily I say unto you that this shall be your reward in the world that now is; and in that which is to come ye shall be with the Ethiopians.

———•♦•———

CHAPTER VIII.

1 *Abraham getteth in trouble with his officers of custom.* 2 *His servant Barney.* 3 *The Tribunes defend him.* 6 *General Raymond of Solferino, organizeth a corps of liars.* 10 *The wickedness of the Times.* 12 *The great General Bust Steed cometh out of the Tombs.* 13 *Day Vis the Traitor.* 14 *Bust Steed draweth a Curtin before him.* 18 *The great General* Cock-Ran. 20 *Dix, who hath an itch for office.* 21 *Daniel the Sickle.* 27 *Rufus, the king's merry-Andrews.*

I. AND Abraham the king shall grow in trouble day by day; for they that serve him shall be of a corrupt heart, insomuch that they shall rob the strong box of the king, and bring his name into great contempt among the people. Even his servant *Barney* shall gather about him, at the receipt of custom, such as traffic with the heathen for their own gain, even Stanton, who is the weak male member of the body of that strong woman, who is the mother of the Bloomers.

II. And they shall make the place of the receipt of customs a den of thieves, so that the merchant men shall murmur among themselves, and shall say unto the king, We pray thee to deliver us from the extortions of thy servant *Barney.*

III. Now the king shall have *Tribunes* in the city of Gotham, at the place of the receipt of customs, which shall rule over the people in his stead; and he shall say to his *Tribunes*, Now judge me of this matter of my servant *Barney*, whether he lacketh anything, or hath too much of his own cunning to be useful unto us.

IV. And the Tribunes shall say unto the king, Thy servant *Barney* is a faithful and just serving-man, inasmuch as he loveth the black Idol, and turneth out of the place of custom all whose grandfathers, yea, whose great-grandfathers were worshippers of the white deities.

V. Then the king shall say, Lo, *Barney* is a good boy.

VI. Now Abraham shall be sorely vexed because of the want of great generals in the land. And he shall send out to the far land of Italy, and command to come unto him the mightiest commander of the world, even General Raymond, the immortal hero of the bloody field of Solferino, and he shall say unto him, I pray thee to organize for me the second great army corps of my kingdom, even an army of *liars*, that we may meet and overcome the worshippers of the white deities, who think to put us down with the TRUTH.

VII. And this mighty general, even Raymond of Solferino, shall hasten unto the king to prostrate himself before the throne; and he shall stand up before the king, in stature a mighty giant, full sixty inches in height.

VIII. And he shall speak to the king, saying, Mighty monarch of the universe! brother to the sun, and first cousin to the moon! behold, both the world and *I* applaud thy wisdom and thy patriotism, in meeting the foolish hosts of *truth* with the proud and the resistless army of *lies*. Thou shalt see how I will scatter them to the four winds of heaven ; yea, they shall be as dust under the wheels of my chariot, so that he that thinketh he standeth by reason of the truth, shall be trodden under foot of the legion of *liars* that I, even Raymond of Solferino, shall lead against him.

IX. And the king shall embrace his liar, even the terrible Raymond, and shall commission him to go forth at once, and smite the armies of truth hip and thigh, so that no man shall dare to tell the truth any more, lest he be thrown into prison, or have his bones broken upon a wheel.

X. Behold, these shall be *Times* that try men's souls !

XI. And Abraham shall appoint him a marshal in Gotham, one Murray, the grammarian, not the son nor the pupil of Lindley; and he shall have a nose like a hound, that smelleth afar the disciples of truth and all such as worship in the temple of the white deities. But he shall be a man without malice, which only executeth the will of the king.

XII. In those days a mighty general shall come up out of the *Tombs* in Gotham, even the great and the invincible Richard the last, called Bust Steed, who is so named because he *bursteth*-away from the ladies' chambers, and rusheth like an unthinking *steed* into battle.

XIII. Him shall the king send forth to meet the armies of *Day Vis*, the Cyclops, who shall be so called because, as his name signifieth, he shall be opposed to the light, and shall seek to delude the minds of his people with sin, even with the darkness and delusion of treason.

XIV. But, lo, when this great general, even *Bust Steed*, shall come into the land of the heathen, the dismayed soldiers of *Day Vis*, the cyclops, shall run before him as hares flee before a tit-mouse, and shall not stop until they have run a hundred thousand miles beyond the gates of their own city, even *Rich Mond*, which is so named in derision, because of the great poverty of the place.

XV. Behold, when the other generals of the king shall see these things, they shall wax jealous of Richard the last, surnamed Bust Steed, and shall persuade the king to send him back to Gotham.

XVI. And Richard the last, when he arriveth in Gotham, shall subside; and he shall seek to hide himself behind a *Curtin*, which cometh from the executive chamber of the land of Penn, but which he findeth at a tavern, where the *Curtin* is wont to be. And this shall be the last of Richard.

XVII. But the feast which Richard the last giveth in honor of the highly illuminated executive *Curtin*, of the land Penn, shall be remembered many days, because of the great and mighty men that shall be there.

XVIII. For unto the feast shall come John, called the General, whose name shall also be Cock-ran, because he goeth into battle like a fighting cock, and runneth out again like a chicken, that hideth itself under its mother's wing when it heareth the cry of the hawk.

XIX. But by reason of these valorous deeds, the worshippers of the Dragon in the land of See More shall make him chief officer of the law, because they shall imagine in their hearts that he who faileth as a general in battle, will make the braver general in peace; and though he knoweth not the law, they shall

take him on their shoulders, and carry him up into the
temple of justice, and set him in the chief seat before
the judges.

XX. And, lo, there cometh among the guests, at the
feast of Richard the last, that other John, whose surname is Dix, who shall become a great general in the
armies of the king, not, withal, because he believeth
in the worship of the Dragon, but because he hath an
itch for office, and is wont to run his head into every
open place where he hopeth to find one.

XXI. Now in those days shall appear Daniel, called
the *Sickle*, because he killeth a man; and he shall be
of such evil report among men, that he seeketh the
battle field that he may die, and be at rest, where he
hideth his sins in the grave.

XXII. But, lo, when he cometh to the battle field,
he shall fight bravely, even standing his ground against
the hosts of the heathen until he loseth a leg; and he
shall not give up until he falleth from his horse by
reason of the loss of much blood.

XXIII. Now when this Daniel returneth to his own
city of Gotham, he shall be of great repute among the
worshippers of the black Idol, insomuch that notwith-
standing aforetime he was hated by the Woolly-heads,
they shall think to put him into the chief seat in
Gotham.

XXIV. By reason of this, great contention shall
spring up among the Woolly-heads, and such as worship
the black Idol in Gotham; and they shall wrangle
among themselves, some saying, What! will you put
this man into the chief seat, who aforetime was offensive
unto us, so that no man trusteth him? Other some
shall say, Hath the cunning vices of the *Sickle's* head
also been lopped off by the losing of a leg?

XXV. But the king's *Tribunes* shall come into the

assembly of the Woolly-heads, and shall command them
to cease wrangling one with another, saying, What
mattereth it who sitteth in the chief seat in Gotham, if
he be a man withal which is void of conscience, so
that he shall not stand up for the law, but willingly
doeth the will of the king?

XXVI. And there shall be silence in the assembly
of the Woolly-heads.

XXVII. But, lo, Rufus, the king's merry-Andrews,
even the surveyor, shall stand up, as he is wont to do,
and blow his own horn, until the people shall run out
of the assembly and scatter themselves to their own
homes.

———•••———

CHAPTER IX.

*3 Stephen rebuketh those who cry war in his name. 4 He denounc-
eth the* Forney-eater. *5 He exposeth Martin, the son of Ryer.
6 And Jacob, the Apostate, surnamed Van Etta. 7 He showeth
how they deceive the people in his name. 9 He prophesieth their
destruction. 14 The people shall break the black Idol in pieces.*

I. AND I, Stephen, saw that there shall be great
tribulation as long as the woolly-headed Dragon liveth.
And many are they that shall fall away from the truth,
and shall speak all manner of lies, and do many un-
clean things in my name, even in the name of Stephen,
the son of Douglas.

II. Behold, such shall go out into the highways,
blowing the trumpet of war in my name. And they
shall say that We are the followers of Stephen, the son
of Douglas, because we are for war; but, verily I say
unto you, that all such shall know that they are deceivers, for there is no truth in them; and they blas-

pheme, and in my name seek the destruction of the land.

III. For did not I say unto the people in the temple of the nation, that " *War is disunion—war is final, eternal separation?*" Did not I proclaim it aloud that, " *Peace is the only policy that can save the country?*" Did not I teach that, " *Only those are for war who want disunion?*" Who, then, are these false teachers that shall go about in my name fanning the red flame of war? Verily I say unto you, they are deceivers, and the sons of darkness, neither is there any truth in them.

IV. And of these deceivers shall be one that sat with me, and break bread at my own table. By reason of his love of filthy lucre he shall sell himself to the king, to be a chief worshipper of the black Idol in the temple of the Dragon. And he shall become fond of strong drink, and shall be given to gluttinous living, and be known in the whole region round about as one that *catereth* to the appetites of his own belly, insomuch that he shall be called *Forney-cater ;* and shall also be called *the dog*, by reason of his much barking for the king.

V. So also shall that Martin, the son of Ryer, who was aforetime a great judge in the kingdom of Jersey, go out falsely teaching war in my name. Him shall Jack the giant-killer slay, so that there shall be heard no more of him, neither of him nor his lies, forever.

VI. And Jacob, the Apostate, also of the kingdom of Jersey, the descendant of the mighty King Gambrenus, the inventor of lager beer, who is surnamed Van Etta, shall bring much scandal upon me by reason of his war howling in my name. Him shall William, called the *Wright man*, by reason of his truth, slay in the Assembly chamber of the kingdom of Jersey; and Daniel,

the Senator, who shall be called Wholes-man, because he is *whole* and hath an undivided heart for
peace, shall bury the apostate, face downward, with
his nose resting upon the first edition of the Helper
Book, because in his lifetime he was a disciple of
Helper, and a secret follower of the Dragon.

VII. Now, all that go out to deceive the people and
teach war in my name shall come to an untimely end,
and perish in the midst of their days; for did I not
stand up in the temple and declare, in the presence of
the traitors who urged the king to go to war, that
" *There is no law that authorizes it. To do the act, or
attempt it, would be one of those high crimes and usur-
pations that would justly subject the President of the
United States to impeachment.*"

VIII. For I say unto you, as was taught aforetime
by the founders of the Republic, even by the mighty
men who framed the Constitution and the Union, and
hath been taught by the Democracy from the beginning, that, " The coercive power of the Federal Government, as applied to States, is the coercion of *law*
and not of *arms.*" Behold, these are the words of the
wise father, speaking in the convention of the States,
even the convention that made the Constitution.

IX. Come, now, hearken unto me; for who is he
that seeth not that, if the chief Government can,
of its own motion, collect an army and send it forth
against the governments of the States, then our fathers
were void of wisdom, nay, they were very fools; for they
thought to form a government of coequal and sovereign
States, when, behold, they made a despotism, even a
military despotism, which hath power at any time to
deluge the land with blood, and bring to an end the
glorious principle of self-government which our fathers
died to establish in this land.

X. Verily I say unto you, that the day cometh that shall bring these men into judgment; for the people shall follow after them in the streets, and shall demand of them, saying, Where is the Union that was builded by our fathers?

XI. And the chief worshippers of the Dragon, even they that aforetime called the Constitution a " lie and a cheat," shall answer them, saying, "The covenant with death" is broken, so that ye can no more have the Union unto yourselves, neither you nor your children, forever.

XII. Behold, when the people shall understand these things, they shall gather themselves together in the market-places, and at the corners of the streets, and, with a loud voice, shall demand of the followers of the king, Give us back the Union that our fathers gave us!

XIII. And the chief rulers shall sneer in their thoughts, and secretly rejoice in their hearts; for they shall think that, by reason of the war, they have sundered the Union, and put an end to the Constitution forever and ever.

XIV. But the people shall grow more and more violent, day by day, insomuch that there shall be great commotion throughout the land, such as never was before in these borders; and they shall rush into the temple of the Dragon and break the black Idol in pieces; and the worshippers of the Idol shall flee before the mighty anger of the people, so that they shall be in fear for their lives, and shall run to and fro, like foxes before the hunter.

CHAPTER X.

Copperhead, Black-snake, and Rattlesnake Indians.

I. And it shall come to pass in those days that the spirit of war shall spread abroad throughout the land, so that every part of it shall be at enmity one with another.

II. Yea, even the Indian tribes that aforetime were at peace with one another, and with all the world, shall be at strife by reason of the wickedness and violence of the worshippers of the Dragon.

III. Lo, the *Copperhead* Indians are brave and generous beyond all other tribes in the land, and seek peace above all things, both with such as dwell in their own land, and such as come from afar.

IV. But the *Black-snake* Indians are of a different tribe; full of all subtlety, yea, of maliciousness, bigotry, revenge, and all uncleanness, insomuch that they can be at peace with no nation, no, not even with themselves.

V. And they shall assemble in their secret places, even in their caves, that shall be called Wide-Awakes, because in them the evil eye never sleepeth; and they shall plot among themselves how they shall get hold of the government, so that they may oppress the *Copperheads*, and destroy the altars that they love, even the altars of the white deities that were builded aforetime by their fathers.

VI. Lo, they shall speak in the secret places to one another, saying, the *Copperheads* are a proud and stiff-necked people, which will never come down to worship the black Idol of our tribe, by reason of the pride of their own birth, and the caste of race, which groweth among them day by day, insomuch that they despise even to enter the temple of the comely black Idol.

VII. Now, therefore, let us make war upon the *Rattlesnake* tribe that inhabit the region that lieth to the south, which is full of riches, and easily tempteth the eye of the stranger, and such as are fond of gain, even of the plunder that cometh of war.

VIII. And, behold, we will cunningly say to the young men of the *Copperheads*, who are brave and full of a martial spirit withal, We pray ye to go down with us and help us against the *Rattlesnakes*, which threaten to descend with fire and sword upon all the tribes of the North, even upon the *Black-snakes* and upon the *Copperheads*, which seek to be at peace with all the world.

IX. And, lo, when the young men of the *Copperheads* shall go down against the *Rattlesnakes*, we will stay behind, even at home, and make ourselves agreeable, if happily we may, to· their wives and ·fair daughters, even to them whose husbands and brothers we have sent off to fight our battles against the tribes of the South.

X. Moreover, when all the young men of the *Copperheads* are away in battle, then will we fall upon their fathers and brothers that shall remain behind, and scourge them, so that they shall not have any peace who refuse to go with us into the temple of the Dragon and worship the black Idol.

XI. And they shall sigh for the Union that their fathers made with all the tribes in this land ; but we will mock at their desires, yea, we will laugh at their expectations ; and when they shall say, let us have the Constitution as it hath been from the beginning, we will smite them, they and the altars of their white deities, so that none shall dare to oppose the new government that the *Black-snakes* shall establish in the land.

———•♦•———

CHAPTER XI.

Great battle between the Snake tribes.

I. BEHOLD, I, Stephen, son of Douglas, saw in my vision the imaginations of the thoughts of the *Black-snakes*, that they were evil continually, and that they will do even as they plotted in the war-councils, in the secret caves of the tribe.

II. And it shall come to pass that the *Copperhead* tribe shall fall into the trap that shall be set for them by the *Black-snake* Indians; and their young men shall go out to battle against the *Rattlesnakes*, even as it was plotted, so that the *Black-snakes* shall be left masters of the situation at home, even of the ballot-boxes, and of the altars of the white deities.

III. But the cunning chiefs of the *Copperheads* shall they bribe with *emeralds*, and with high posts of honor, both in the temple of the Dragon and the army that moveth against the tribes of the South.

IV. So that these, even the *Copperhead* chiefs, which shall sell themselves for *emeralds* or office, shall be the most daring and devilish of all the conspirators in the temple of the Dragon; yea, they shall be put foremost by the chiefs of the *Black-snakes*, to smite the altars of the white deities wherever they shall find them, and to bring to an end both the Constitution and laws that have been in this land from the beginning.

V. But it shall come to pass that the widows and orphans of the *Copperheads* that shall be slain in the battles of the *Black-snakes*, shall be an exceeding great throng, so that they shall block up the streets, and hinder men and women from passing to and fro freely to the churches and market-places.

VI. And these, even the widows and orphans, shall cry aloud in the streets, and shall demand of the rulers of the *Black-snakes*, and of the apostate chiefs of the *Copperheads*, Where are our husbands? where are our fathers?

VII. But the rulers of the *Black-snakes* and the apostate chiefs of the *Copperheads* shall answer them nothing.

VIII. And the flood of death, even the tide of blood, shall roll on until it hath covered the whole land, so that the angel of destruction shall sit at every man's door, and the bloody banner of the *Black-snakes* shall wave over the fallen altars of the white deities in the temple of liberty.

IX. And it shall come to pass that when the old men, and the virtuous youths, of the *Copperheads* shall see these things they shall begin to murmur among themselves, saying, To what end is this sea of blood? and who hath bewitched our people that they join the *Black-snakes* against their own race?

X. Then the rulers of the *Black-snakes* shall seize upon all such, and thrust them into prison to be devoured of the woolly-headed Dragon.

XI. Verily, I say unto you, that all this shall only make matters the worse for the *Black-snakes* and their Idol; for the *Copperheads*, though they be a peaceful tribe, shall be wrought in the extreme by reason of these oppressions, and they shall begin to say one to another, Now, why have we permitted these things?

XII. For is not this the land of our fathers? and this temple of liberty, was it not builded by their hands? and these altars of the white deities, were they not established for us, and for our children forever?

XIII. Now, therefore, why do we permit all these things to be destroyed under the cheat of making war upon the *Rattlesnakes* of Sunland?

XIV. For doth it come to pass that we cannot fight the *Rattlesnakes* afar in Sunland, without beating our own altars to pieces at home? Must we give up our own liberty and become the slaves of the *Black-snakes*, for the sake of depriving the *Rattlesnake* tribe of their freedom?

XV. And, behold, when the *Black-snakes* shall hear and understand these murmurings among the *Copperheads*, they shall wriggle, and squirm, and hiss, and begin to put themselves in the attitude to spring upon the *Copperheads*, and shall threaten to strangle them.

XVI. Now the *Copperheads* are armed with a deadly weapon, so that when their enemies, even the *Black-snakes*, shall fall upon them, they will meet with swift destruction.

XVII. And the battle when it cometh shall be short, and the end of the *Black-snakes* shall be as sudden as the lightning falleth out of the clouds.

XVIII. For the whole tribe of the *Copperheads* are warriors; and when their enemies shall fall upon them, who have, withal, few brave warriors of their tribe, they shall drive them like chaff before a mighty rushing wind, yea, and they shall be scattered as chaff to the four winds of heaven.

XIX. And I, Stephen, Son of Douglas, see that the end of these things shall be that the *Black-snakes* shall be driven into their holes, and their Idol in the temple of the Dragon shall be broken in pieces, so that the white deities, whose altars are in the temple of liberty, shall abide in this land forever and ever.

END OF BOOK FIRST.

www.ingramcontent.com/pod-product-compliance
Lightning Source LLC
Chambersburg PA
CBHW031819090426
42739CB00008B/1341